THE ECLIPSE
OF EXCELLENCE

THE ECLIPSE
OF EXCELLENCE

A Critique of
American Higher Education

By STEVEN M. CAHN

Foreword by Charles Frankel

Resource *Publications*
An imprint of *Wipf and Stock Publishers*
199 West 8th Avenue • Eugene OR 97401

To Richard Taylor

A Friend

Resource Publications
An imprint of Wipf and Stock Publishers
199 West 8th Avenue, Suite 3
Eugene, Oregon 97401

The Eclipse of Excellence
The Incisive Critique of American Higher Education
By Cahn, Steven M.
Copyright©1973 by Cahn, Steven M.
ISBN: 1-59244-534-9
Publication date 2/3/2004
Previously published by Public Affairs Press, 1973

FOREWORD

Colleges and universities surely have as high a proportion of lost souls on their faculties as do most other human institutions, but the word has got around, nonetheless, that it is the function of colleges and universities to save souls, showing them the way to salvation, emotional, erotic, mystical. Colleges and universities are notoriously places where administration is jumbled and politics mean, yet the word has got around that it is at centers of higher learning that the political vision exists which can save the rest of the nation. Colleges and universities are enormously expensive, yet the theory has captured many minds that there is nothing one can learn on a campus that one couldn't learn better off it, and that the classroom and laboratory are monuments to irrelevance from which the People must by all means be saved.

These notions, when set down in straight English, are manifestly absurd. They have won their victory by becoming associated with the ideas of youth, healthly discontent, and unwillingness to compromise with a shoddy educational status quo. It is, therefore, a refreshing and promising event when an accomplished young philosopher and dedicated teacher like Professor Cahn turns his mind to the present crisis in higher education and concentrates on some home truths.

Professor Cahn has his eyes on the future, not the past. He is as full of divine discontent as of contemporaries of his who have acquired a certain flash fame, and he has much more humility. But most important of all, he is concentrating, in this wise and unpretentious little book, on the staple realities of teaching and liberal learning rather than on labels, packaging, cant slogans and messianic expectations.

The subjects on which Professor Cahn writes—classroom standards, examinations, grades, the selection of disciplines to study, the mastery of definite materials that have an independent existence outside one's ego—may seem, from the standpoint of the fashionable educational theories, almost too petty to consider. To talk about education without giving them the unapologetic and serious attention which Professor Cahn does is like discussing anatomy while spending only a few moments in passing on the heart, kidney, lungs, and joints. Professor Cahn's book is unusual if only because he does not think himself too profound to take elementary material problems into account. But he shows, good philosopher that he is, that this is perfectly compatible with demanding expectations for education and with an imaginative understanding of its purposes and possibilities.

Here is a book which it is a pleasure to commend as a restorative of common sense and, hopefully, of a sense of common educational purposes.

CHARLES FRANKEL

CONTENTS

"University recently abolished all distribution requirements, except for 2-course sequence in English (unless waived) . . . Since 1969-70 up to half of 32 courses for graduation may be taken pass/fail—more with approval of the major department." (American University, Washington, D. C.)

"Brown has now eliminated all distribution requirements . . . and allows 'satisfactory' or 'no credit' grades for all courses. No course failure becomes part of student record; only 28 courses required for graduation." (Brown University, Providence, Rhode Island)

"Basic requirements have been dropped . . . . New grading system offers choice between graded and ungraded for each course . . . . no failing grade appears on record." (Hobart and William Smith Colleges, Geneva, New York)

"A student leader recently characterized the situation at Lawrence: 'Academic revolution has taken place in the last 2 years. Distribution requirements have been dropped . . . There is a program that lets you do your own thing . . . student-designed courses, tutorials, independent study, etc'." (Lawrence University, Appleton, Wisconsin)

"Requirements for graduation have been very significantly relaxed in the past 3 or 4 years . . . Grading is optional satisfactory/unsatisfactory for up to half the courses . . ." (Macalester College, St. Paul, Minnesota)

"All general requirements for graduation have been eliminated . . . Satisfactory/unsatisfactory grading system for freshmen and sophomores." (State University of New York at Albany, New York)

From the *Comparative Guide to American Colleges*, fifth edition (1972) by James Cass and Max Birnbaum

CHAPTER 1

INTRODUCTION

American higher education stands on the brink of chaos. Never have so many spent so long learning so little.

Years ago the majority of students who went to college faced a serious intellectual struggle. If they were to succeed academically, they had to spend long hours preparing for their courses. Even to obtain the so-called "gentleman's C" required considerable effort. Professors challenged a student's fundamental beliefs and commitments, and if he was to maintain pride in himself, a student had to respond to these challenges. Moreover, an individual's fellow students were often unimpressed with his views and forced him to defend hasty generalizations and retreat from oversimplified positions. In short, a student's college experience was once intellectually meaningful.

Unfortunately such is not the case today. Instead, for the majority of students college has become a mere social adventure. A minimum of study is required, for if a college still gives grades—and many no longer do—they are awarded so liberally it is relatively easy to do well and virtually impossible to fail. Professors on the whole do little teaching, and most would prefer to do even less. Their major concern seems to be either advancing professionally or ingratiating themselves with those they are supposed to be instructing. And one's fellow students? They are more interested in attacking the administration politically than in challenging one another intellectually. The focus of their attention is not schoolwork but world problems, problems whose solutions require the very understanding that is the product of a rigorous education. But most students seek to avoid such an education; they erroneously assume it irrelevant to their concerns and apparently no one, including their teachers, is willing to disabuse them of their fantasies. Thus, although a college diploma may still be of use, one cannot say the same for a college education.

The saddest feature of the entire situation is that so many teachers and administrators no longer have faith in the educational process or in themselves. Lacking all sense of purpose and oblivious to the value of their own intellectual training, those responsible for educational policy have lost their way—and, very possibly, their courage. Their decisions have been made not in an effort to improve education, but in an effort to appease student pressure. The tendency has been to abandon requirements, abandon examinations, abandon grades—in brief, to abandon all educational standards. What is happening on the nation's campuses is that in the name of student freedom, excellence is being disdained and mediocrity glorified, personal achievement downgraded and aimless, useless activity applauded. In short, due to weakness in leadership, our colleges have fallen prey to intellectual barbarism.

The longer we continue to offer our students an empty education, the greater becomes the threat to our society, for the most dangerous enemy of a democracy is the ignorance of its citizens. Yet we must ask ourselves what sort of higher education is appropriate for those who are members of a democracy. Can such education be carried out in accordance with the highest intellectual standards? If so, how? These are the critical questions this book attempts to answer.

CHAPTER 2

THE CONTENT OF A LIBERAL EDUCATION

Education is the acquisition of knowledge, skills, and values. But what is the knowledge, what are the skills, and what are the values that ought to be acquired? The answers to these questions are clearly of the utmost importance, for they form the foundation upon which a person builds his life. No man, however, is an isolated being. Each life is intertwined with many other lives, and the welfare of a democratic society ultimately depends upon decisions made by all members of the community. A proper education is the key to making wise decisions. And the ingredients of this education are our first concern.

In a democracy where all adult citizens are supposed to participate in the decision-making process, each individual's education should be of equal concern. A democracy that neglects the education of some will pay a dear price, for the enemies of freedom feed upon ignorance, fear, and prejudice. Thus if an individual should complain his democracy is providing too much education for too many people, he reveals his ignorance about the very nature of democratic process; indeed, too little education and there may soon be no democracy.

Equal concern for each person's education does not mean providing each person with exactly the same education. Rather it means providing each person with appropriate educational opportunities. Individuals differ in their capacities and interests; what stimulates one person may stultify another. A democracy should recognize such differences and show equal consideration for all persons by enabling each to enjoy his own distinctive growth. "In proportion to the development to his individuality," as John Stuart Mill pointed out, "each person becomes more valuable to himself, and is therefore capable of being more valuable to others." [1]

However, just as it is important to recognize the need for individuality within a democracy, so we must recognize the need for all citizens to possess certain attributes in common. Indeed, an examination of the most important of these attributes will disclose the essential elements of a proper education for free men in a free society.

Let us begin such an examination by noting the obvious fact that all members of a democracy should be able to read, write, and speak effectively. An individual who is unable to understand others or to make himself understood is both hindered in his personal growth and unable to participate fully in the free exchange of ideas so vital to the democratic process. A command of language is indispensable for such an exchange, and so it is of vital importance for members of a democracy to acquire linguistic facility.

Also necessary is an understanding of public issues. How can a citizen participate intelligently in the discussion of an issue he does not understand? Furthermore, how can he intelligently evaluate the decisions of his representatives if he is unable to comprehend the complexities of the questions they are deciding? Public issues in a democracy cover an enormous range of topics, for every action taken by the government is a subject for public discussion, and such actions typically involve social, political, economic, scientific, and historical factors. Consider some of the critical issues confronting the world today: overpopulation, poverty, pollution, racial conflict, ideological conflict, the dangers of nuclear warfare, and the possible benefits of space research. How can these issues be judged or even understood by those ignorant of the physical structure of the world, the forces that shape society, or the ideas and events which form the background of present crises? Thus substantial knowledge of natural science, social science, world history, and national history is required for all those who are called upon to think about public issues, and in a democracy such thinking is required of everyone. Granted, elected representatives must carry the major burden of formulating and implementing governmental policies. Still each citizen has both the right and the duty to evaluate and try to influence the decisions of his government.

Of course, knowledge of science requires familarity with the fundamental concepts and techniques of mathematics, since mathematical notions play not only a critical role in the natural sciences but also an ever-increasing role in the social sciences. Furthermore, apart from its use in other areas of study, mathematics is itself an invaluable aid in the handling of everyday affairs, for, as Alfred North Whitehead noted: "Through and through the world is infected with quantity. To talk sense, is to talk in quantities. It is no use saying that the nation is large,—How Large? It is no use saying that radium is scarce,—How Scarce? You cannot evade quantity." [2]

However, to know the results of scientific and historical investigations is not sufficient; one must also understand the methods of inquiry that have produced those results. No amount of knowledge brings intellectual sophistication, unless one also possesses the power of critical thinking. To think critically is to think in accord with the canons of logic and scientific method, and such thinking provides needed protection against the lure of simplistic dogmas that appear attractive, yet threaten to cut the lifeline of reason and stifle the intellect. A member of a democracy who cannot spot a fallacious argument or recognize relevant evidence for a hypothesis is defenseless against those who would twist facts to suit their own purpose.

Still another characteristic should be possessed by all members of a democracy: sensitivity to aesthetic experience. Such experience is, to use John Dewey's words, "a manifestation, a record and celebration of the life of a civilization, a means of promoting its development, and is also the ultimate judgment upon the quality of a civilization." [3] An appreciation and understanding of the literature, art, and music of various cultures enriches the imagination, refines the sensibilities, deepens feelings, and provides increased awareness of the world in which we live. We should never forget that in a society of aesthetic illiterates not only the quality of art suffers but also the quality of life.

We should also note in connection with the study of literature that significant value is derived from reading some foreign literature in its original language. Not only does great literature lose some of its richness in translation, but learning another language increases linguistic sensitivity and makes one more conscious of the unique potentialities and limitations of any particular tongue. Such study is also a most effective means of widening cultural horizons, for understanding another language is a key to understanding another culture.

One further element is requisite to a liberal education: a knowledge of human values. Aristotle recognized long ago that virtue is of two kinds, what he termed "moral virtue" and "intellectual virtue." Moral virtue, which we might call "goodness of character," is formed by habit. One becomes good by doing good. Repeated acts of justice and self-control result in a just, self-controlled person who not only performs just and self-controlled actions but does so, in Aristotle's words, "from a firm and unchangeable character." [4] Of course, moral virtue is not acquired primarily through formal schooling. A school cannot be expected to instill decent behavior in those whose moral education has been disregarded or mangled by family and community.

Intellectual virtue, on the other hand, is what we might refer to as "wisdom." In a narrow sense, a wise man is one who is a good judge

of value. He can distinguish worth from cost. He possesses discern-
ment, discretion, and an abundance of that most precious of qualities,
common sense. Wisdom, in this sense, is acquired partly as a result
of habit, partly as a result of informal teaching, and partly perhaps, as
the ancient Greeks would have said, as a gift of the gods.

But in a broader sense a wise man is one who possesses intellectual
perspective, who is familiar with both the foundations of knowledge
and its heights, who can analyze the fundamental principles of thought
and action while maintaining a view of the world that encompasses
both what is and what ought to be. Such wisdom is of inestimable
value to members of a free society, for it enables them to stand firm
in the face of intellectual challenge and hold fast against those who
would first entrap the minds of free men and then enslave their bodies.
The path to wisdom in this sense lies in the study of those great
visions that comprise philosophy.

It should be clear now that education within a democracy must not
be limited to training individuals in occupational skills, for no matter
what occupation a member of a democracy may choose, he will be called
upon to take part in decisions of public policy, and his education must
be broad enough to enable him to make such decisions wisely. Among
the Romans such a broad education was permitted only to freemen
(in Latin: *liberi*), and therefore this education is today appropriately
referred to as a "liberal education."

We would make a grave misjudgment, however, if we assumed liberal
education unrelated to vocational education. If the members of a
democracy are to be not only knowledgeable participants in the political arena but also effective contributors in the social sphere, each
citizen should be provided with the necessary skills, social orientation,
and intellectual perspective to succeed in some broad field of occupational endeavor. But such a vocational education must not be confused
with narrow job-training. Animals are broken in and trained; human
beings ought to be enlightened and educated. An individual ignorant
of the aims of his actions is unable to adjust these actions in the face
of changing conditions, and he is thus stymied by a world in flux. As
Sidney Hook has noted, "There is a paradox connected with vocational
training. The more vocational it is, the narrower it is; the narrower it
is the less likely it is to serve usefully in earning a living . . . there
is no reason—except unfamiliarity with the idea—why vocational education should not be liberated to include the study of social, economic,
historical, and ethical questions . . ." [5] For the sake of the future

worker as well as for the benefit of his society, such liberalized vocational preparation should be included in the spectrum of a liberal
education.

At this point it is well to consider the widely discussed question:
Is a liberal education any longer relevant? "Relevant" is one of those
terms so aptly described by the philosopher J. L. Austin as "snakes in
the linguistic grass" used "without caution or definition or any limit,
until it becomes, first perhaps obscurely metaphorical, but ultimately
meaningless." [6] Nowadays "relevant" seems to wriggle into every
conceivable context, although it rarely possesses any clear-cut sense.
The only practical way to deal with such a word is to distinguish its
various possible meanings and then consider how each would affect the
sense of the issue under consideration.

Sometimes "relevant" is used to mean "topical." In this sense a
study is relevant if by chance it deals with current matters. Thus
a course in Greek tragedy or the history of the United States would
not be relevant, whereas a course dealing with today's avant-garde
dramatists or contemporary racial conflict in America would be. But
to use the word "relevant" this way is to confuse what is topical with
what is timely. The plays of Sophocles were topical only during the
golden age of Athens, but they are timely in every age, for they never
lose their power to enrich human experience and deepen our response to
life. Slaves in America were freed by 1865, but an understanding of
the lives they lived prior to that time is crucial to an understanding
of current racial problems. To confine a liberal education to
what is topical would exclude much material of value to all members of
a democracy. Therefore, if "relevant" is taken to be synonymous with
"topical," relevance ought not be a criterion for deciding the content
of a liberal education.

However, the word "relevant" is not always used in this sense,
Occasionally it refers to any subject concerned with the nature, origin,
or solution of the fundamental social, political, intellectual, or moral
problems of our time. In this sense a liberal education *should* be
relevant, for its very purpose is to enable citizens of a free society to
make wise decisions about the problems that confront them.

But in order to apply this notion of "relevance" without distortion,
it is necessary to clarify its potentially misleading aspects. First, not
every problem of our time is a fundamental problem. An education
that fails to analyze the nature of capitalism but concentrates instead
upon devising plans to increase sales in a local store will not provide

the intellectual perspective required to understand economic decisions taken by the government. Of course, it might be useful to examine capitalism from the standpoint of a local storeowner, but not so narrowly as to lose sight of the broader picture a liberal education ought to provide.

Second, experiencing the actual situation in which a problem arises does not by itself guarantee increased understanding of the problem. Field study can be a valuable tool in learning, but it should be structured so as to enable a student to acquire knowledge or skills requisite to a liberal education, and some reasonable means should be employed to determine how much the student has learned. Insight into fundamental problems is not gained simply by immersion in the stream of experience. Indeed, some experiences may engender laxity or carelessness and do more to impede learning than foster it.

Third, some subject matters and skills not directly related to any specific contemporary problems are nevertheless crucial to a liberal education, since they form the basis for an intelligent approach to all problems. As we have seen, without linguistic and mathematical facility, without the power of critical thinking, without aesthetic sensitivity and philosophical perspective, it would be impossible to deal adequately with the fundamental problems of our time.

Fourth, concentration upon contemporary issues may result in a failure to recognize how inextricably they are tied to the past and how much can be learned about them through a study of the past. The urgencies of present problems should not mislead us into believing it a waste of time to consider the past, for in order to know where you are going, it is advantageous to know where you have been.

With these four clarifications in mind, and remembering the meaning we have given "relevant," we can safely say the liberal education we have described is and should be relevant.

Our examination of the word "relevant" is not completed yet, for the word is used in still another sense, namely, as a synonym for "interesting." A subject of study is relevant only if one happens to find it absorbing, and a subject relevant to one person may not be relevant to another. According to this definition, is a liberal education relevant? No doubt to some people it is and to others it is not. But should an individual's education be restricted to what he finds relevant?

The one way to ensure that people will always be interested in what they are being taught is to teach them only what interests them. If a person enjoys history but not science, then he is taught history and not science. And if he is bored by most history but fascinated by the history of the American cowboy, then he is taught that history and nothing else. Such an education would unquestionably be relevant, that is, interesting, but it would not achieve the aim of a liberal education. It would not equip members of a democracy to carry out their obligations as citizens in a free society. And this aim is not an arbitrary one, for the success of a democracy ultimately depends upon the education of its citizens, and it is in each person's interest to live within an enlightened, democratic society. Thus education should not be restricted to what an individual happens to find relevant, for he may not be interested in gaining mastery of certain knowledge and skills indispensable to all members of a democracy.

It would be a serious mistake, however, to assume that because an individual's education should not be restricted to what he finds interesting, it is unimportant whether he is interested in what he is learning. An involved, attentive learner unquestionably derives far greater benefit than one who is bored and inattentive. We have seen it would be a major error to stimulate the learner by teaching him only what interests him. How then should his attention be aroused and maintained?

There are basically two possible answers to this critical question. One, which might appropriately be labeled the traditional view, is that the learner's interest should be engaged by the external pressures of reward and punishment. The other, the fundamental principle of what has come to be known as the "progressive" view, is that the learner's interest should be engaged by presenting material in such a way that it connects with the learner's own experience, with his own aims and purposes; the material itself thereby becomes the learner's personal concern. Of course, to engage the learner's interest through the promise of reward and the threat of punishment invites an obvious danger, for if that interest remains dependent upon external influences the termination of these influences may cause the termination of the learner's interest, and thus he may fail to develop a most important quality, the desire to continue learning. Therefore, as much as possible, it is advantageous to focus the learner's interest directly on the material itself. But this goal is hardly easy to accomplish, and finding means of doing so is one of the most important and difficult challenges facing any teacher. Indeed, it is so demanding one is tempted to escape it by falling back upon the easy device of allowing the learner's interest to dictate the material he is taught. But to succumb to this temptation is, as we have seen, a fatal blunder. Every attempt should be made to render the content of a liberal education relevant, i.e. interesting, but to do so by abandoning the proper content is to repair the ship by sinking it.

Unfortunately, such sinkings have become all too common in our colleges today, and so it is most important we be able to recognize such disasters when they occur and learn to avoid them. How to do so is the next subject for consideration.

1. John Stuart Mill, *On Liberty* (New York: The Liberal Arts Press, 1956), p. 76.

2. Alfred North Whitehead, *The Aims of Education and Other Essays* (New York: The Free Press, 1967), p. 7.

3. John Dewey, *Art As Experience* (New York: Minton, Balch & Co., 1934), p. 326.

4. Aristotle, *Nicomachean Ethics*, trans. Martin Ostwald (New York: The Bobbs-Merrill Company, 1962), 1105a, 34.

5. Sidney Hook, *Education for Modern Man: A New Perspective* (New York: Alfred A. Knopf, 1963), pp. 203, 207.

6. J. L. Austin, *Sense and Sensibilia* (Oxford: The Clarendon Press, 1962), p. 15. For those who are interested in the study of snaky words (a study which might properly be called "verbal ophiology"), I suggest the following specimens: objective, subjective, natural, absolute, relative, pragmatic, and existential.

CHAPTER 3

THE MYTH OF THE ROYAL ROAD

Euclid, the Greek mathematician, was once asked whether there was an easy way to master his monumental geometric treatise, the *Elements*. His answer: "There is no royal road to geometry." What Euclid said about geometry might equally be applied to every branch of serious human endeavor. Whether one sets out to become skilled at cooking, golf, violin-playing, or chemistry, there is no royal road to mastery.

It is easy to have great ambitions. What is difficult is to fulfill them. So many of us go through life aware of our talents and abilities but somehow never really developing them. We are left consoling ourselves with the thought, "I could have if only . . ."

One example of such undeveloped talent often comes to my mind. Many years ago I happened to attend a summer camp that had a strong athletic program. Although many good athletes were there, one in particular stood out. He was only fifteen years old, but already his athletic prowess was remarkable. Since he possessed few interests outside sports and because baseball was the game he loved most of all, everyone assumed he would one day be a major league star.

I heard nothing further about him until several years ago when I saw him at a camp reunion. He was playing in an old-timer's baseball game and quite naturally was the object of everyone's attention. He was still by far the best player but now overweight and considerably slower than in his camp days. Later I talked with him and asked what he had been doing. As it turned out, he had played in the minor leagues for a short while but soon had given up baseball and become a construction worker. His voice was quiet, as of one whose dream had long since faded.

When I asked a counselor at the camp who had known him all his life how such a superb athlete could have failed, this was the reply: "I know he loved to play baseball, but that's all he would do— play it. He wasn't willing to work at it. Fielding ground balls at training camp may be fun for an hour, but by the second hour the fun disappears; by the third hour the strain begins to tell and the field empties. By the fourth hour just a few men are still practicing. They're the only ones who have a real chance to be major leaguers. The rest better find something else to do."

That ability to work the counselor mentioned, aptly termed "self-discipline," was felicitously described by John Dewey as "power at command . . . a power to endure in an intelligently chosen course in face of distraction, confusion, and difficulty." [1] It is a prime requisite for the achievement of worthwhile goals, for, as noted previously, the road to mastering any significant skill is not an easy one. Distractions, confusions, and difficulties abound. Only the individual who persists in the face of such obstacles can succeed, and talent will not suffice where self-discipline is lacking.

The present crisis in American higher education is very largely the result of attempting to provide students with a sound liberal education without requiring of them the necessary self-discipline and hard work. Students have been led to believe they can achieve without effort, that all they need do in order to obtain a good education is skip merrily down the royal road to learning. The catch, however, is that what appears to be a royal road to learning is no more than a detour to the dead end of ignorance.

We must realize that becoming an educated person is a difficult, demanding enterprise. A man would be thought foolish if he spoke of intense physical training as a continuous source of joy, delight, and ecstasy, for we all know how much pain and frustration such training involves. A man should be thought equally foolish if he speaks of intense mental exertion as a continuous source of joy, delight, and ecstasy, for such effort also involves pain and frustration. It is painful to have one's ignorance exposed, and it is frustrating to be baffled by intellectual subtleties. Of course, there is joy in learning just as there is joy in sport. But the joy in both cases is a result of overcoming rigorous challenges, and such joy cannot be experienced without toil.

It is not easy to read intelligently and think precisely. It is not easy to speak fluently and write clearly. It is not easy to study a subject carefully and know it thoroughly. But these abilities are the foundation of a sound education. As Jacques Barzun has noted, "Of what use to even an unusually bright pupil are all the visual aids, paperback books, field trips, documentary movies, special lectures, and 'opportunities for independent work' if he lacks the categories of thought and habits of study which would enable his impressions to cohere?" [2]

If an individual is to become educated, he must learn that although every member of a democratic society is equally entitled to express his opinions, not all expressed opinions are equally sound. Some claims are true, some false. Some arguments are valid, some invalid. Some hypotheses are well-founded, some not. A student must learn that maintaining and defending an intellectual position is not the same as choosing a favorite color. Some positions are self-contradictory, some run counter to the available evidence, and some are so vague it is unclear what they mean or whether they mean anything at all. An educated man does not simply believe; he believes what he can explain and cogently defend.

If a student is to learn intellectual responsibility, he must be taught to recognize that not every piece of work is a good piece of work. In fact, some work is just no good at all. A student may be friendly, co-operative, and even sensitive to the needs of mankind, but he may nevertheless turn in a muddled economics paper or an incompetently researched laboratory report. And that he means well is no reason why he should not be criticized for an inadequate performance. But such criticism is rare nowadays. As John Searle has pointed out, "In the universities one sees a growing reluctance to insist on a high level of performance even from those who are capable of producing it. The current pretense that spontaneous and sincere incompetence is acceptable manages to demean both the teacher and the pupil." [3]

Some educators, however, fear that if a student's work is criticized and he is forced to work harder, he will come to hate what he is studying and consequently learn nothing. Of course, a student may be criticized in such a way that he no longer has any desire to continue learning, and such destructive criticism must be avoided. But there is such a thing as constructive criticism that makes clear to a student his work is not what it should be, yet at the same time stimulates him to try harder, do better, and learn more. It is one thing to say to a student, "Your work is awful. Why are you so stupid?" It is quite another to say, "You haven't yet caught on to the technique of writing clearly, and you're just not communicating what you want to say. Try again and I'm sure if you're more careful, you can do much better." The first sort of criticism is to be avoided. But the second sort is vital to intellectual growth, for an educated person must be able to recognize the difference between clarity and obscurity, accuracy and carelessness, knowledge and ignorance.

And yet despite the fact that obtaining a sound liberal education is such a hard task, the majority of today's students do well in their college courses with relative ease. In fact, a recent front-page article in *The New York Times* indicated college grades are rising steadily and at an accelerating rate throughout the country. At Northwestern University, for example, the rise has been from an average grade of C in 1967 to an average grade of B in 1971. Correspondingly, far fewer students are failing out or being put on academic probation. At the University of Illinois, for instance, during the 1964-65 academic year 16 per cent of the undergraduates were dropped or placed on probation; in 1971 the figure was less than 4 per cent. And this pattern applies to all schools, public and private, large and small, urban and rural. As one senior at the University of Wisconsin put it, "I never go to school any more, and I still get wonderful grades. There's a common consensus here that it's a lot easier to get good grades." [4] The obvious implication of rising grades at a time when barriers to attending college are being lowered is that comparatively few of our colleges are fulfilling their vital function in a democratic society: providing their students with a sound liberal education. What specifically accounts for this failure? Just why do students find their college work such an empty challenge?

The source of much of the problem is the increasingly widespread acceptance among faculty and administrators of the erroneous and dangerous educational principle that a student should not be required to do any academic work he would prefer not to do. According to this principle, which is coming more and more to dominate the educational policy of our colleges, if a student prefers not to study science or history or literature, he can attain his degree without studying any science, history, or literature. If he prefers not to take examinations he can either make special arrangements with his instructor or else choose his courses from among the ever-increasing number that involve no examinations. If he prefers that his work not be graded, he can arrange in many or all of his courses to receive an undifferentiated pass or fail. Indeed, some schools now offer courses impossible to fail. Attendance is not required, examinations are not required, papers are not required. Nothing is required. Registering for the course guarantees academic credit. The day may not be far off when a high-school student's acceptance to college ensures his college diploma. Is it any wonder, then, students find it easy to do college work? The only wonder is that any work at all is still going on.

Why is this trend prevalent? More specifically, why has the principle of student license been so easily accepted? In my view, those educators who have not acquiesced in this matter solely out of fear of student reprisals have done so at least in part because they have forgotten the educational justification for structuring a student's course of study. Requirements, examinations, and grades have for so long been virtually uncontested aspects of higher education that their existence has required no defense. But, as John Stuart Mill remarked, unless a widely accepted opinion is "vigorously and earnestly contested, it will, by most of those who receive it, be held in the manner of a prejudice, with little comprehension or feeling of its rational grounds. And not only this, but . . . the meaning of the doctrine itself will be in danger of being lost. . ."[5] Such has been the fate of the doctrines supporting rigorous educational structure.

The time has come to remind ourselves of the grounds for making demands on students and to expose the fallacious thinking underlying the myth of the royal road. Vindication has already been provided for requiring students in a liberal arts college to master a wide variety of knowledge and skills. But why should a college education involve examinations and grades? That is the crucial question to which we turn next.

1. John Dewey, *Democracy and Education,* (New York: The Free Press, 1966) p. 129.

2. Jacques Barzun, *The House of Intellect* (New York: Harper & Row, 1959), p. 112.

3. John Searle, *The Campus War* (New York and Cleveland: The World Publishing Company, 1971), p. 242.

4. Iver Peterson, "Flunking is Harder as College Grades Rise Rapidly," *The New York Times* (March 13, 1972), p. 1.

5. Mill, p. 64.

CHAPTER 4

THE CASE FOR EXAMINATIONS AND GRADES

It is astonishing to realize how little a college teacher may know about the academic lives of his students, and conversely, how little his students may know about the academic life of their teacher. I recall one professor who taught a large lecture course for several years without ever realizing he was addressing a captive audience, since, unbeknownst to him, the course was required for graduation. On the other hand, I have spoken to students unaware that just as a student can be required to take a course he would prefer not to take, so a teacher can be required to teach a course he would prefer not to teach. How many teachers, even in a very small class, know whether their students are sophomores or seniors, a matter of some importance to the students? But again, how many students know whether their teacher is an assistant or full professor, a matter of some importance to the teacher? It may never occur to a teacher that the sleepy students in his 8 a.m. class are there only because all other sections of the course were already closed when they registered. But, likewise, it may never occur to the students in the 8 a.m. class that their teacher is standing wearily before them at such an hour only because he lacks the seniority to claim any other time.

Such mutual ignorance extends over many aspects of academic life and is nowhere more apparent than in matters regarding examinations and grades. A basic source of the misunderstandings which surround evaluations of student work lies in the fact that normally such evaluation has vital consequences for the one being evaluated, whereas it has no such consequences for the one who does the evaluating. The grades a student receives not only determine whether he graduates with honors or fails out of school; they may also guide him in choosing his field of specialization, affect his plans for graduate study, and ultimately influence his choice of career. On the other hand, the grades a teacher gives do not affect his professional stature, his commitment to a field of study, or his future success as a scholar. A student may for a long time harbor a deep resentment against a teacher who grades him harshly, but were he to confront that teacher years later, the teacher might not even remember the student and would almost surely not remember the grade. Indeed, the teacher would most probably be astounded to learn the student cared so deeply about the grade. I once heard a woman who had taught for over thirty years remark in a faculty meeting that she could not understand why students were so interested in grades. Apparently in moving from one side of the desk to the other she had developed amnesia.

Some students believe that teachers are fond of examinations and grades, that they employ these devices in order to retain power over the students. But although undoubtedly a few teachers do possess such motives, most do not. A scholar enjoys reading and writing books, not making up questions to test the knowledge of students. And a great many more fascinating things can be found to do than read one hundred or so answers to the same question and try to decide how many points each answer is worth. Whether Johnny understands the problem of induction is not crucial to Professor Smith's intellectual life, for Professor Smith finds the problem highly stimulating, even if Johnny neglects to study it.

The system of examinations and grades thus places important decisions affecting students' lives in the hands of those who are comparatively unaffected by these decisions and perhaps quite uninterested in making them. Such a situation is fraught with unpleasant possibilities, these often compounded by the difficulty of constructing and applying suitable examination and grading procedures. But to refer to "suitable examination and grading procedures" implies that such procedures are intended to fulfill certain worthwhile purposes, and so we would do well at this point to consider just what those purposes are. In other words, why bother with examinations or grades at all?

Examinations ideally serve at least four significant purposes. First, an examination provides the opportunity for a student to discover the scope and depth of his knowledge. Much like an athlete who tests himself under game conditions or like a violinist who tests himself under concert conditions, a student tests himself under examination conditions and thereby determines whether he is in complete control of certain material or whether he possesses merely a tenuous grasp of it. It is one thing to speak glibly about a subject; it is something else to answer specific questions about that subject, relying solely upon one's own knowledge and committing answers to paper so they can be scrutinized by experts in the field. A proper examination procedure makes clear to the student what he knows and what he does not know and thus can serve as a valuable guide to further study. By paying close attention to the results of his examination, a student can become aware of his strengths and weaknesses. He can learn whether his methods of study are effective, and he can recognize the areas of a subject in which he needs to concentrate his future efforts. In short, an examination enables a student to find out how well he is doing and assists him in deciding how he can do better.

Students, however, are not the only ones who are tested by an examination, for the second purpose examinations should serve is to provide an opportunity for a teacher to discover how effective his teaching has been. By carefully analyzing his students' examination papers, a teacher can learn in what ways he has succeeded and in what ways he has failed. Of course, many teachers would prefer to believe the reason three-quarters of their students missed a particular question is that the students are not bright or have not studied hard enough. But in this matter, college teachers have something to learn from those who teach in elementary school. When three-quarters of an ordinary third-grade class find multiplication confusing, the teacher does not assume the students are not bright or have not studied hard enough. He assumes his teaching methods are in need of improvement. A college teacher ought to arrive at the same conclusion when three-quarters of his class are confused by a fundamental point he thought he had explained clearly. In one sense, then, teachers as well as students can pass or fail examinations, for by paying close attention to the results of his students' efforts, a teacher can become aware of the strengths and weaknesses of his instruction. He can learn whether his methods are effective, and he can recognize the areas of a subject in which he needs to concentrate his future efforts. In short, an examination enables a teacher to find out how well he is doing and assists him in deciding how he can do better.

We have thus far considered examinations only as tests of learning, but they can be more than a means of evaluating previous learning experiences: they can be themselves worthwhile learning experiences. During an examination most students are working with an extraordinarily high degree of concentration. If the examination questions place familiar material in a slightly unfamiliar light and thereby lead students to develop for themselves significant connections between various aspects of the subject matter, then the students will be working intensely on challenging, important problems and so gain intellectual perspective. Ironically, in this day of large lecture classes, examinations sometimes provide greater opportunity for active learning than any other part of the course. It is not unusual to hear student complaints about uninspired, unrewarding examinations. Such complaints are entirely legitimate, for a boring, banal examination indicates pedagogic laziness and is a waste of a potentially valuable learning experience. Long after completing a course, students who have forgotten virtually everything else may still remember some of the examination questions. They should be worth remembering.

An examination, however, consists of more than the two or three hours spent sitting in the examination room. Most students prepare for examinations, and such prepartion itself possesses significant educational value. The nature of an examination requires that one not know what questions will be asked or which aspects of the subject matter spotlighted. The only adequate preparation for an examination is a thorough study of all the subject matter and a careful consideration of as many as possible of its various interconnections. In trying to anticipate the examination questions, a student is led to analyze and synthesize the course material, thereby strengthening and solidifying his grasp of the subject matter.

In this connection it is important to note that the writing of a term paper, though potentially a beneficial educational experience, is not a suitable substitute for preparing for an examination. In writing a term paper, even one which is given a strict time limit and misleadingly dubbed "a take-home examination," a student needs only master those parts of the course material bearing directly on his topic. Rarely does a term paper require mastery of most or even very much of the course material. Furthermore, it is not difficult to copy ideas from a book, alter them slightly so as to avoid the charge of plagiarism, and use them in a term paper without ever thoroughly understanding them. Such a tactic is almost impossible in an examination, for few students have a strong enough memory to answer questions intelligently without understanding their answers. Thus, preparing for an examination is in some ways, though not all, more demanding and more rewarding than writing a term paper.

This fact was strikingly brought to my attention several years ago by a student who came to see me after I had returned her examination paper. She had received a C and was very disappointed, for, as she explained, she had always been an A student. I asked her whether she had studied as hard for this examination as for previous ones, and to my surprise she informed me that never before in her academic career had she taken an examination. As it turned out, she had gone to a "progressive" secondary school where examinations were considered outmoded, and she had then attended a college that prided itself on having replaced all examinations with term papers. I was fascinated by this woman's academic background and inquired whether she thought she had been helped or hindered by it. She replied that until she had taken this examination she had always assumed it was to her advantage to have avoided the pressure of examinations, but that now she believed her grasp of previous course material rather flimsy. She had learned how to write term papers but never had thoroughly mastered an entire body of material so that she could draw upon it at will and utilize it effectively wherever it was called for. In short, she had never received the benefits of preparing for an examination.

Of course, examinations serve yet another purpose, for they are in part the basis on which course grades are determined. However, since we have already seen that examinations provide an opportunity to discover the scope and depth of a student's knowledge, we have little reason to doubt that if grades are to be given, they should be based, at least to some extent, on the results of examinations. The crucial question is: why should grades be given?

Ideally, a grade represents an expert's opinion of the quality of a student's work within a specified area of inquiry. Viewed in this perspective, a grade serves a variety of significant educational purposes. First, it is to a student's advantage to be aware of his level of achievement, for that information can be a valuable aid to him in assessing his past efforts, evaluating his present abilities, and formulating his future plans. Knowing whether one's approach to a subject has been fruitful is a helpful guide toward further study; recognizing one's strengths and weaknesses is vital to intellectual growth as well as to decisions regarding how one's abilities might most effectively be utilized in and out of school. A college student is directly concerned with questions such as "Which courses should I take?", "Which fields should I specialize in?", "Which graduate schools, if any, should I apply to?", and "Which career should I choose?" Intelligent answers to all these questions depend, among other factors, upon the individual's academic abilities and accomplishments, and he can measure these reliably, though not infallibly, by his grades. Granted a teacher's judgment may occasionally be mistaken, at least his judgment is based upon relevant expertise and experience and is not subject to the sort of delusions which so often distort self-evaluation. A student may not always be pleased by the knowledge grades afford, but the important point is that such knowledge is almost always useful to him.

Students, though, are not the only ones to whom such knowledge is useful, for in order for a teacher to provide the detailed educational advice often so helpful to a student, he needs to have an exact record of the student's academic performance. How can a teacher intelligently advise a student in choosing his program of study and in planning for the years after graduation if an accurate measure of the student's level of achievement is unavailable? If, for example, a chemistry teacher does not know how well a student has done in his various science and mathematics courses, how can the teacher intelligently advise the student which level of chemistry to study, which areas in the student's background need strengthening, and whether it is reasonable for the student to continue work in graduate school? And if the student should decide to become a political science major, how can a teacher in that discipline intelligently advise the student what course of study to follow without knowing his level of achievement in history, economics, sociology, philosophy, and nowadays even in mathematics? In short, students' academic records are a great aid to those teachers who try to use their knowledge and experience to advise students wisely. But if a student's record is sketchy, vague, and inadequate, the advice he receives will most likely also be sketchy, vague, and inadequate.

We have already noted that grades can be a valuable guide to a student in planning for the years following his graduation, but we should note as well that grades are a valuable guide to those who must make critical decisions directly affecting a student's future plans. Graduate work usually presupposes a firm command of undergraduate work, and thus most graduate schools necessarily employ selective admission policies. Those who face the difficult task of deciding whether a particular student is to be admitted to graduate school can make that decision intelligently only if they are aware of the student's level of achievement in his various college courses, and grades are a reliable, though not infallible, measure of such achievement.

On occasion, however, it is proposed that instead of receiving an applicant's grades a graduate admissions committee receive instead recommendations written by each of the teachers with whom the applicant has studied. But this proposal is impractical and, even if feasible, would nevertheless be inadvisable.

The proposal is impractical for at least two reasons. First, the members of an admissions committee do not have the time to read twenty-five or thirty letters about each applicant. In the case of some of the larger graduate schools, an admissions committee with twenty-five letters for each applicant would be facing more than twenty-five thousand letters and could not possibly be expected to spend the time necessary to do justice to that amount of material. Second, the large size of so many college classes makes it virtually impossible for a teacher to know each of his students personally. Thus he would be reduced to writing such convential comments as "DeWitt is an excellent student who has mastered all of the course material" or "Davis is a fair student who has mastered some, though not much of the course material." But what do these comments mean except that DeWitt did A work in the course and Davis did C work?

However, even if it were feasible for every one of a student's teachers to write a personalized comment about him and for an admissions committee to read all of these comments, still they would not be an adequate replacement for grades. Recommendations sometimes contain valuable information, but taken by themselves they are often difficult to evaluate. A remark one teacher considers high praise may be used indiscriminately by another, and a comment employed by one teacher to express mild commendation may be used by another teacher to express mild criticism.[1] Furthermore, many recommendations are hopelessly vague and tell more about the teacher's literary style than about the academic accomplishment of the student. Thus although letters of recommendation may be helpful when used in conjunction with grades, alone they are no substitute for the relatively standardized measure of achievement grades effectively provide.

Such a standardized measure of achievement also affords a reasonable basis upon which to decide whether a student ought to be permitted to continue in school, whether he ought to be granted a college degree, and whether he ought to be awarded academic honors. These decisions, however, have all been the subject of controversy, and so we would do well to consider each of them separately.

A student who consistently does unsatisfactory work is squandering the resources of his college, wasting the time and energy of his teachers, and failing to contribute to, perhaps even interfering with, the education of his classmates. Such a student does not belong in the school he is attending, and, for the benefit of all concerned, should be asked to leave. But which students are doing unsatisfactory work?

In answering this question it is clearly most sensible to rely upon the expert judgment of the faculty, and their judgment, as noted previously, is reliably reflected by a student's grades.

The faculty's expertise ought also to be relied upon in deciding whether the quality of a student's work justifies his being granted a college degree. Because most students are charged tuition fees, it is tempting to conceive of a college as an educational store in which the student customers pay their money and are then entitled to a degree. But a college degree is not purchased; it is earned. It represents to the community the college's certification of a student's academic achievement, certification respected because it is backed by the expertise of the faculty. If every student who paid his tuition automatically received a degree, or if degrees were awarded by the vote of the student body, then they would become educationally meaningless and functionally worthless. In order for a college degree to retain its value and for a college education to retain its significance, the granting of degrees must be based solely upon substantial academic achievement as evaluated by recognized experts. The experts are the faculty, and their evaluations are indicated by the grades they give.

Grades also provide an effective means of determining which students are deserving of academic honors. Such honors are both an added incentive for students to pursue their work diligently and a symbol of a college's commitment to academic excellence. But in order for honors to possess such significance, they must not be granted indiscriminately or on the basis of a student's popularity. Rather, they must be awarded only to those who have attained a high level of scholarly achievement. And grades provide a standardized measure of such achievement.

Grades serve one final purpose: to motivate students to study. In the classroom, as in most areas of life, those who expect their work to be evaluated tend to do that work more assiduously. Without grades, many students might possess sufficient interest to casually peruse the course material, but few would be strongly enough concerned to devote themselves to the mastery of that material. Of course, there are a handful of students who would thoroughly study all of their course material even if they did not receive any grades. These are the saints of the academic world. But a teacher should no more assume all his students saints, than he should assume all his neighbors saints. In both cases he would do well to hope for the best but prepare for the worst. What should be remembered is that grades have helped many students who otherwise would have neglected their work, and have led some to discover for themselves the intrinsic joys of scholarship.

We must recognize, however, that notwithstanding the many worthwhile purposes examinations and grades are intended to fulfill, much criticism has been directed against these educational tools. It has been claimed that examinations fail to provide a sound basis for evaluating a student's achievement but, instead, have the effect of inhibiting his independence and stifling his creativity. It has also been claimed that grades are inherently inaccurate devices which, in attempting to measure people, succeed only in traumatizing and dehumanizing them. These charges are certainly serious, and each of them ought to be examined in detail.

Consider first the claim that examinations do not provide a sound basis for evaluating a student's achievement. Those who defend this claim argue that examinations require a student to demonstrate his knowledge under adverse conditions; he must answer a restricted set of questions within a limited amount of time, and the implicit pressure prevents many from doing their best work. Thus the results of examinations are said to be invalid.

But this line of argument overlooks the vital consideration that although examinations put pressure on students, such pressure exists whenever an individual attempt to prove to experts his competence in their field. For instance, an athlete feels pressure when he tries out for a professional team; likewise a violinist when he auditions for an orchestral position. Pressure is inherent in such situations, for experts have high standards difficult to meet, and one must be able to meet those standards at an appointed time. The ballplayer who appears skillful in practice but plays poorly in league games lacks effective control of the requisite skills. Similarly, the student who sounds knowledgeable in conversation but performs poorly under examination conditions lacks effective control of the requisite knowledge. Thus the pressure of examinations does not invalidate the results of examinations; quite to the contrary, if there were no such pressure, the examination process would be amiss.

A second criticism of examinations is that they inhibit a student's independence, that they discourage him from pursuing topics of interest to him and instead force him to study topics of interest to his teacher. Thus, it is said, examinations impede rather than promote the learning process.

This criticism, however, rests upon the mistaken assumption that learning a particular subject matter involves nothing more than learning those aspects of the subject matter one happens to find interesting. For example, to attain a thorough knowledge of American history, it is not sufficient to learn the history of the American Indian, no matter how interested one may be in the Indians, for American history, like any significant area of inquiry, has many important aspects, all of which must be mastered in order to attain a thorough knowledge of the field. But who is to decide which aspects of a subject matter are most important? The teacher is the recognized expert, and so he is in a position to make intelligent curricular decisions. Furthermore, the teacher's responsibility is to use his expertise to further a student's education, to guide him in studying important aspects of the subject matter he might otherwise neglect. Such guidance, in one sense, interferes with a student's independence, but in another, more significant, sense, liberates him from his own narrow preoccupations and leads him to less restricted, more independent thinking. And that, after all, is one of the essential purposes of a liberal education.

Another criticism of examinations is that they stifle a student's creativity, that they emphasize the mindless reiteration of facts and techniques instead of encouraging original, imaginative thinking about significant issues. Thus, again it is said, examinations impede rather than promote the learning process.

But this criticism is mistaken for at least two reasons. First, not all examinations emphasize learning by rote, only poor examinations. Good examinations, as pointed out previously, place familiar material in a slightly unfamiliar light, so that in preparing for and taking examinations, students are led to develop for themselves significant connections between various aspects of the subject matter. Of course, an examination does not normally require the same degree of original, imaginative thinking required by a demanding term paper topic. But it must be remembered a term paper does not require mastery of most or even very much of the course material; only examinations do. In other words, the two tasks serve different purposes, and there is no point in criticizing one for not fulfilling the purposes of the other.

The second reason why the criticism in question is mistaken is that it overlooks that in order to master any significant field of inquiry, one must acquire secure control of certain fundamental information and skills. As Whitehead wrote, "There is no getting away from the fact that things have been found out, and that to be effective in the modern world you must have a core of definite acquirement of the best practice. To write poetry you must study metre: and to build bridges you must be learned in the strength of material. Even the Hebrew prophets had learned to write, probably in those days requiring no mean effort. The untutored art of genius is—in the words of the Prayer Book—a vain thing, fondly invented." [2] It is simply unrealistic to suppose that original, imaginative thinking of a sustained and productive sort flows from the minds of those ignorant of the fundamental information and skills related to their field of inquiry. Of course, it has been said that the mark of a knowledgeable person is not what he knows, but whether he is adept at looking up what he needs to know. But if this were so, then the most knowledgeable people in the world would be librarians. The fact is a person who lacks fundamental information and skills is not in a position to understand and intelligently evaluate material confronting him, so he is unable to connect ideas in the ways necessary for sustained, productive thinking. And even if, as is highly doubtful, such an individual had the time to research everthing he needed to know, he would not know what to research, for he would not be aware of all he needed to know. But how can it be determined whether an individual possesses the fundamental information and skills related to his field of inquiry? Examinations enable both teacher and student to make such determinations effectively, and thus, rather than stifling creativity, help to provide the framework within which original, imaginative thinking can be most productive.

Turning now from criticisms of examinations to criticisms of grades, consider first the claim that grades are inherently inaccurate. Those who defend this position argue that the same paper would be graded differently by different instructors, and therefore a student's grade is not a reliable measure of his achievement but merely indicates the particular bias of his instructor.

However, a student's work is generally not judged with significant difference by different instructors. In fact, teachers in the same discipline usually agree as to which students are doing outstanding work, which are doing good work, which are doing fair work, which are doing poor work, and which are doing unsatisfactory work (or no work at all). [3] Of course, two competent instructors may offer divergent evaluations of the same piece of work. But the fact that experts sometimes disagree is not, of course, reason to assume there is no such thing as expertise. For example, two competent doctors may offer divergent diagnoses of the same condition, but their disagreement does not imply that doctors' diagnoses are in general biased and unreliable. Similarly, two competent art critics may offer divergent evaluations of the same work of art, but such a disagreement does not imply that a critic's evaluations are usually biased and unreliable. Inevitably, experts, like all human beings, will sometimes disagree about complex judgments, but we would be foolish to allow such disagreements to obscure the obvious fact that in any established field of inquiry some individuals are knowledgeable and others are not. And clearly the opinions of those who are knowledgeable are the most reliable measure of an individual's achievement in that field. Thus, although teachers sometimes disagree, they are knowledgeable individuals whose grades represent a reliable measure of a student's level of achievement.

A second criticism of grades is that they traumatize students. Those who support this criticism argue that grades foster competition, arousing a bitterness and hostility which transform an otherwise tranquil academic atmosphere into a pressure-filled, nerve-wracking situation unsuited for genuine learning. In such a situation, it is said, students are more worried about obtaining good grades than about obtaining a good education.

But this criticism emphasizes only the possibly harmful effects of competition while overlooking its beneficial effects. Often only by competing with others do we bring out the best in ourselves. As Gilbert Highet once noted, "It is sad, sometimes, to see a potentially brilliant pupil slouching through his work, sulky and willful, wasting his time and thought on trifles, because he has no real equals in his own class; and it is heartening to see how quickly, when a rival is transferred from another section or enters from another school, the first boy will find a fierce joy in learning and a real purpose in life." [4] In short, competition fosters excellence, and without that challenge most of us would be satisfied with accomplishing far less than we are capable of.

However, even if competition did not have beneficial effects, it would still be an inherent part of academic life, for it is an inherent part of virtually every aspect of life. Many people have the same goals, but only a comparatively few can achieve them. For example, not everyone who so desires can be a surgeon, a lawyer, an engineer, or a professional football player, and, indeed, marked success in any field of endeavor is necessarily quite rare. Thus competition arises. And since academic success is desired not only for its own sake but also because it relates to success in many other competitive fields, competition will always exist in academic life.

The question then is not whether competition should be eliminated from the academic sphere, but how it can be channelled so as to maximize beneficial effects and minimize potentially harmful effects. The key to this difficult task lies in encouraging each student to strive as vigorously as possible to fulfill his own potential, in praising his efforts when he tries his hardest and in appealing to his sense of pride when his energies flag. Treating him so does not lead him to emphasize good grades rather than a good education, for he cannot achieve a good education without striving for mastery of subject matter. And if grades are awarded as they should be, on the basis of accurate measures of a student's level of achievement, then they will indicate his mastery of subject matter. Thus a student concerned with grades is concerned with a prime component of a good education.

A third criticism of grades is that in attempting to measure people, they succeed only in dehumanizing and categorizing them, depriving them of their uniqueness, and reducing them to a letter of the alphabet. Thus, it is said, grades defeat one of the essential purposes of an education: to aid each individual in developing his individuality.

A grade, however, is not and is not intended to be a measure of a person. It is, rather, a measure of a person's level of achievement in a particular course of study. To give a student a C in an introductory physics course is not to say that the student is a C person with a C personality or C moral character, only that he is a person with a C level of achievement in introductory physics.

Grades no more reduce students to letters than batting averages reduce baseball players to numbers. That Ted Williams had a lifetime batting average of .344 and Joe Garagiola an average of .257 does not mean Williams is a better person than Garagiola, but only that Williams was a better hitter. And why does it dehumanize either man to recoginze that one was a better hitter than the other?

Indeed, to recognize an individual's strengths and weaknesses, to know his areas of expertise, his areas of competence, and his areas of ignorance is not to deny but to emphasize his individuality. If

Delaney and Delancey are known to their teachers only as two faces in the classroom, then their comparative anonymity is apt to lead to their individual differences being overlooked. But if Delaney has a reputation as an excellent history student with a weakness in mathematics, while Delancey is known as a generally poor student, but one who has a gift for creative writing, then these two students are no longer anonymous cogs in a machine, and their education can be tailored to suit their needs. Thus grades do not dehumanize an individual; on the contrary, they contribute to a recognition of his uniqueness and to the possible development of his individual interests and abilities.

Yet there is one further challenge to the entire system of examinations and grades, for as was pointed out earlier in the chapter, this system places important decisions affecting students' lives in the hands of those comparatively unaffected by these decisions and perhaps quite uninterested in making them. Such a situation is indeed hazardous, and the potential problems are, of course, compounded by the difficulty of constructing and applying suitable examination and grading procedures. Of course, suitable procedures are the ones most likely to fulfill the worthwhile purposes examinations and grades are intended to serve, and we have already seen what those are. But what specifically are the procedures most likely to fulfill those purposes? And how can it be ensured that teachers will be cognizant of the proper procedures and apply them conscientiously? These are important questions, and they deserve careful consideration.

Constructing a good examination is a creative endeavor, and, as in the case of all creative endeavors, there are no surefire formulas for success; the most one can reasonably hope for are broad guidelines to provide a sound basis for at least partial success. The first such guideline is that an examination should be representative of the course material. Consider, for instance, a course in the history of modern philosophy that devotes two or three weeks to the study of each of five philosophers: Descartes, Leibniz, Berkeley, Hume, and Kant. If the final examination is to serve its proper function as a test of the scope and depth of a student's knowledge of the course material, then the examination should be structured so that a student is called upon to demonstrate considerable knowledge about all five of the authors studied. The examination would be unsatisfactory if it tested only a student's general philosophical ability, not his knowledge of the five authors studied, or if it tested a student's knowledge of only one or two authors studied and permitted him to neglect the others. For whatever such unsatisfactory examinations might be intended to test, they would fail to test adequately the scope and depth of a student's knowledge of the history of modern philosophy.

Of course, an examination representative of the course material need not deny students a choice as to which examination questions they wish to answer. Such a choice is an attractive feature of an examination, since it allows students an opportunity to demonstrate their special interests and abilities. But the crucial point is that such choices should be so arranged that a student's answers will adequately reflect his knowledge of the entire course material. And if certain course material is so essential that all students should be familiar with it, then no choice should be given. For contrary to common practice, students need not always be offered a choice of examination questions. What they should be offered is an examination representative of the course material.

A second guideline for constructing good examinations is posing questions that require detailed answers. Perhaps the most serious fault of college examinations is that they allow a student to talk around the subject matter without ever having to demonstrate more than a superficial knowledge of the course material. Again in contrast to common practice, much can be said in favor of questions that have answers, answers to be found in or at least closely related to the course readings. An examination lacking such questions is not merely a poor test of a student's knowledge but leads him to suppose that thorough knowledge of the course material amounts to no more than knowing a few stray bits of information strung together by some vague generalizations about some even vaguer concepts. Such an examination is worse than no examination at all; it is an educational travesty that leads a student to suppose he has mastered material about which he knows virtually nothing.

But the fact that examination questions ought to require detailed answers is no reason why students should be overwhelmed with true-false or multiple-choice questions. Through these can sometimes be of educational value, unless they are well-constructed and appropriate to the aims of the course, they turn the examination into a guessing-game that stresses knowledge of minutiae rather than the understanding of fundamental concepts and principles. For instance, only a foolish examination in the history of modern philosophy would be filled with questions such as "The title of Section IX of Hume's *An Inquiry Concerning Human Understanding* is (a) Of Liberty and Necessity, (b) Of the Reason of Animals, (c) Of Miracles, (d) All of the above, (e) None of the above." On the other hand it would be equally foolish for such an examination to be filled with questions such as "Does it seem to you that anything in the work of Kant helps us to understand ourselves?" What is needed is neither a trivial nor vague question but a sharply defined, significant, challenging question, one such as: "Both Descartes and Berkeley raise doubts about the existence of the material world. Compare and contrast (1) the arguments they use to raise these doubts, and (2) their conclusions concerning the possible resolution of these doubts." An examination with questions such as this not only provides a rigorous test of a student's knowledge but also clearly indicates to the student that mastery of the subject matter is a demanding enterprise, requiring far more intellectual effort than the memorization of trivia or the improvisation of hazy, high-flown vacuities.

If an examination adheres to the two important guidelines just discussed, then there is reason to suppose it will fulfill the worthwhile purposes it should serve. However, several other pitfalls must be avoided in order for an examination to be as effective as possible. First, the examination should not be so long that most students are more worried about finishing than about providing the best possible answers. Of course, if a student takes too long to answer a question, it is clear he does not have secure enough control of the required material. But basically an examination should not be a race against time; it should be constructed so a student working at a normal pace has sufficient time to read the questions carefully, compose his thoughts, write his answers legibly, and reread his work to make corrections. No matter how well-constructed examination questions may be, if there is not sufficient time to answer them thoughtfully, then the examination will turn into a shambles and be of little use to anyone.

A second pitfall to be avoided is the omission of clear directions at the top of the examination paper. Imagine sitting down to begin work and reading the following directions: "Answer three questions from Part I and two questions from Part II, but do not answer questions 2, 3, and 6 unless you also answer question 9. Question 1 is required, unless you answer questions 3 and 5." By the time a student has fully understood these directions and decided which questions he ought to answer, he will already be short of time.

When a student sits down to take an examination, he is understandably tense and liable to misread the directions, answer the wrong questions, and bungle the examination. If he does so, the fault is probably not his, for the teacher has the responsibility to make the directions so clear that the student will find them virtually impossible to misunderstand. A teacher has sufficient time to work out clear directions, and he owes it to his students to provide such directions. The examination should be a test of a student's knowledge of the course material, not a test of his ability to solve verbal puzzles.

A third pitfall is the failure to inform students of the relative importance of each answer in the grading of the examination. Suppose a student begins work on an examination in which he is required to answer three questions, but is not told the teacher considers the answer to the third question more important than the combined answers to the first two. The student will probably spend an equal amount of time on each, never realizing he should concentrate his time and effort on the third. But his mistake indicates no lack of knowledge on his part. It is simply a result of the teacher's keeping his own intentions a secret. And this secret serves no other function than to distort the results of the examination. It is only fair that a student be informed as to how many points each question is worth, so that he can plan his work accordingly.

One final pitfall must be avoided in order for an examination to fulfill its proper purposes, and this pitfall relates not to the construction of the examination, but to its grading. A teacher is responsible for grading examinations as carefully and fairly as possible. To do otherwise is to waste much of the effort put into constructing and taking the examination, for an examination graded carelessly or unfairly does not provide an accurate measure of a student's knowledge. Of course, the most essential element in the proper grading of examination papers is the teacher's serious effort to carry out his responsibility conscientiously, but many teachers have found a few simple suggestions about grading techniques helpful. First, a teacher should grade papers without knowing whose paper he is grading. An answer from a student who does generally good work is apt to seem more impressive than the same answer from a student who does generally poor work. Next, it is best not to grade a paper by reading it from start to finish but to read and grade all students' answers to one question at a time. This procedure ensures that a teacher will pay attention to each answer a student gives and not skim the paper after reading only the first one or two answers carefully. Furthermore, correcting papers in this way makes much less likely the possibility a teacher will alter his standards as he moves from one paper to another, for it is far easier to stabilize standards for answers to the same question than for entire examination papers. Finally, before grading a question, a teacher should list for himself the major points he expects students to mention in their answers. He can then check each essay against this list, providing yet another safeguard against altering standards as he moves from one paper to another. And such a list also provides a teacher with the means to justify his grades, since he is in a position to indicate to students what a good answer should be. Such information makes clear that grades have not been meted out arbitrarily and also aids each student in achieving both a better understanding of the material tested and an increased awareness of his own strengths and weaknesses. Of course, in order for such information to be most useful, examinations should be graded, returned to students, and discussed in class as soon as possible after being given.

Examinations that adhere to these guidelines and avoid these pitfalls are almost sure to be reasonably successful examinations. It should be kept in mind, however, that good examinations reinforce one another, since each examination a student takes guides him in future study. Thus if he takes a number of good examinations in a single course, as that course proceeds he learns how to derive the greatest possible benefit from his study time. Multiple examinations in a single course also serve to discourage students from the popular but disastrous policy of wasting almost the entire term and then cramming for one final examination. The more frequent the examinations, the less need for cramming. Thus it is not, as some have said, that examinations encourage cramming. Infrequent examinations encourage cramming. Frequent examinations encourage studying. And good examinations encourage useful studying.

Having now discussed suitable examination procedures, we should next consider suitable grading procedures. Much discussion has taken place about alternative grading systems, but the basic principle for constructing an effective grading system remains quite simple: it should contain the maximum number of grade levels teachers can use consistently. A grading system should be as specific as possible because grades serve as a guide for the educational decisions of both students and faculty: up to a reasonable point the more detailed the guide is, the more helpful it is. If a student's academic record is sketchy and vague, then most likely he will have a sketchy, vague idea of his own abilities and accomplishments and will be hindered in his attempts to assess his past efforts, evaluate his present capabilities, and formulate his future plans. And not only will he himself be hindered, but those who try to advise him or evaluate his accomplishments will be at a serious disadvantage. It is just not sufficient to know that Kubersky passed a course. Was he an A student, a strong B student, a weak C student, or a D student? Without an answer to this question, neither Kubersky nor anyone else knows much about his level of achievement.

But there is a limit to how specific a grading system should be. Ultimately we reach a point where no reasonable basis exists for deciding whether a student's work is at one level or another. There is little sense, for example, in trying to decide whether an English composition should receive a grade of 86.32 or 86.31, for no teacher can consistently differentiate between work on these two levels.

The question is then, using the principle that a grading system should contain the maximum number of grade levels teachers can use consistently, how many such grade levels should there be? My own experience has led me to believe that in college the most effective grading system is the traditional one, consisting of ten symbols: A, A-, B+, B, B-, C+, C, C-, D, F. This ten-level system is specific enough to provide the needed information about a student's level of achievement while enabling teachers to differentiate consistently between work on any two of the ten levels. Of course, borderline cases will sometimes arise, but the distinction between work on any two levels is clear, despite the possibility of borderline cases, just as the distinction between bald men and hirsute men is clear, despite the possibility of borderline cases.

Perhaps the most controversial aspect of the traditional ten-level system is its grade of F, for many have claimed that if a student knows he will have a failure permanently on his record, he may become so discouraged he will give up on his education altogether. In order to preclude such a possibility it has been proposed that the grade of F be replaced by a grade of NC (No Credit), which would indicate to the registrar both that the student should receive no credit for the course and that his transcript should show no record of his having taken the course.

Such a grade, however, would obviously be pure deception, for the student *did* take the course and he failed to master any significant part of it. If he should take the same course again and pass it, his transcript should indicate as much. Otherwise, those who are trying to evaluate his work will be mislead, since, for example, it is likely a student who had to take introductory chemistry two, three, or four times before passing lacks the scientific or study skill of someone who passed the course on his first try. It is not a tragedy to fail a course, but it is a failure, and we must learn from failures, not give them another name and pretend they did not occur. Indeed, one mark of a mature individual is facing up to and taking responsibility for failures. As a colleague of mine once remarked during a faculty meeting in which the NC grade was being discussed: "When I die and stand before the Heavenly Judge in order to have my life evaluated, it may be that I will receive a grade of F. But let it not be said that my life was a 'No Credit'."

A suitable grading system, however, does not ensure suitable grading, for unless the system is used properly, grades will not achieve the worthwhile purposes they are intended to serve. And, unfortunately, improper uses of the system are all too common.

One such misuse is to award grades on bases other than a student's level of achievement in the course work. Irrelevant bases for grades include a student's sex, race, religion, nationality, physical appearance, dress, personality, attitudes, innate capacities, and previous academic record. None of these factors should even be considered in awarding grades. To repeat what was said earlier, a grade ought not to be a measure of a person; it ought to be a measure of a person's level of achievement in a particular course of study, and the only reasonable basis for measuring this is the quality of work which he does in that course.

The most effective way for a teacher to assure his students that no extraneous factors will enter into the awarding of grades is to state clearly at the outset of the term exactly how final grades will be determined. How much will the final examination count? How much will short quizzes count? How about the term paper and other shorter papers? Will laboratory work count? Will a student's participation in class discussion be a factor? By answering these questions at the very beginning of the course, a teacher sets a student's mind at ease and, in addition, enables him to concentrate his time and effort on the most important aspects of the course. Of course, some teachers assume that if they do not discuss their grading policy, the students will not worry about grades. But quite to the contrary, a teacher's failure to discuss his grading policy increases uncertainty and worry and furthermore provides no guidance as to how the students should work to do their best and get the most out of the course. And, after all, such guidance is precisely what the teacher is expected to provide.

A second obvious misuse of the grading system, exceedingly rare nowadays, results from the reluctance of some teachers to award high grades. Such teachers pride themselves on how rarely they give an A or B, and how frequently they give C's, D's, or F's. But low grading is a foolish source of pride, for such grading suggests the teacher is unable to recognize good work when he sees it. That a student's work does not deserve immortal fame is no reason it does not deserve an A. Just as a third-grade student who receives an A in writing need not be the literary equal of a college student who receives an A in English composition, so a college student who receives an A in English composition need not be the literary equal of Jonathan Swift or Bertrand Russell. Giving a student an A in a course does not mean he has learned everything there is to know about course material or that he is as knowledgeable as his teacher; giving a student an A simply means that, considering what could reasonably be expected, the student has done excellent work. If a third-grade teacher rarely gives an A or a B, his principal does not assume this teacher always has poor students in his classes. He assumes, rather, that this teacher has a distorted sense of academic values. A similar conclusion should be reached about a college teacher who rarely gives an A or a B. Such a teacher is misapplying the grading symbols and preventing grades from fulfilling their important educational functions.

A third misuse of the grading system, one especially prevalent today, results from the reluctance of many teachers to award low grades. These instructors pride themselves on never giving students a hard time or underestimating the value of a student's efforts. But high grading, like low grading, is a foolish source of pride; it suggests that the teacher is unable to recognize poor work when he sees it. Not to differentiate between two students, one doing poor or unsatisfactor work and one doing fair work, is a subtle form of discrimination against the better student. Giving a student a D or an F in a course does not mean that the student is a foolish or evil person; the low grade simply means that, considering what could reasonably be expected, the student has done poor or unsatisfactory work. If a third-grade teacher rarely gives low grades, his principal does not assume this teacher has the school's most brilliant students. The principal assumes, rather, that this teacher is giving his seal of approval to incompetent work. A similar conclusion should be reached about a college teacher who rarely gives low grades. Such a teacher, like the teacher who rarely gives high grades, is misapplying the grading symbols and preventing grades from fulfilling their functions.

A fourth and final misuse of the grading system is the practice commonly referred to as "grading on a curve." The essence of this widely adopted practice is deciding what percentage of students in a class will receive a particular grade, without considering the level of work actually done by any of the students. For example, a teacher may decide before a course ever begins that 10 per cent of the students will receive an A, 20 per cent a B, 40 per cent a C, 20 percent a D, and 10 per cent an F. Distributing grades in this way produces an aesthetically pleasing curve on a graph, but the procedure is invalid, for how well a student has learned a particular subject matter does not depend upon how well his fellow students have learned the same subject matter. Perhaps in many large classes approximately 10 per cent of the students actually do A work and a similar percentage F work, but this fact is no reason at all why in any specific class exactly 10 per cent of the students must receive an A and another 10 per cent must receive an F. Suppose 25 per cent of the students in a class do excellent work and 5 per cent unsatisfactory work; then the 25 per cent should receive an A and the 5 per cent an F. Or suppose 5 per cent of the students in a class do excellent work and 25 per cent do unsatisfactory work; then the 5 per cent should receive an A and the 25 per cent should receive an F. For the grade a student receives is not to be a measure of his rank in class; it is to be a measure of his level of achievement in a particular course of study. And though judging a student's level of achievement does depend upon considering what can reasonably be expected of him, such a judgment does not and should not depend upon the level of achievement of other students who happen to be taking the same course simultaneously. Since the Procrustean practice of grading on a curve rests upon such irrelevant considerations, the practice ought to be abandoned.

Having now provided an answer to the question, "what specifically are suitable examination and grading procedures?", only one question remains for consideration: how can it be ensured that teachers will be cognizant of suitable examination and grading procedures and apply them conscientiously? The answer to the first part of this question is for those who administer graduate school programs to provide courses in methods of teaching for students intending to enter the teaching profession. These courses should be required of all students who are to be recommended for teaching positions and should include a detailed discussion of suitable examination and grading procedures. The person chosen to teach such a course ought to be himself a productive scholar and an outstanding teacher, for he is in the best possible position to make clear to graduate students that good scholarship and good teaching are not incompatible, that publishing develops a teacher's ability to think critically by leading him to submit his ideas to the judgment of his peers, while teaching encourages a scholar to express his views clearly enough to communicate them effectively to those not as knowledgeable as he.

But even if a teacher is cognizant of suitable examinations and grading procedures, how can it be ensured he will apply them conscientiously? There is, of course, no practical way to ensure that anyone whether doctor, journalist, or taxi driver, will do his job conscientiously. A departmental chairman has the responsibility to make certain no member of his department is guilty of gross negligence. But, ultimately, a teacher must decide for himself whether to be conscientious. If he is deeply committed to maintaining high academic standards, he will be willing to spend the time and effort required to make the most effective possible use of examinations and grades. But if he is unconcerned about promoting excellence and is satisfied with exalting mediocrity, he will be unwilling to give of himself in order to provide his students with effective examinations and accurate grades. What no teacher must be allowed to forget, however, is that if he chooses to ignore proper examination and grading procedures, both his students and his society will be the losers.

1. Grade designations, however, are few in number and have a relatively standardized meaning. Therefore, teachers who use them idiosyncratically are not the victims of linguistic ambiguity but of pedagogic inadequacy.

2. Whitehead, p. 34.

3. These five levels of work are commonly symbolized by the letters: A, B, C, D, F. Teachers who misuse these symbols are an educational menace; their sins are discussed later in the chapter.

4. Gilbert Highet, *The Art of Teaching* (New York: Vintage Books, 1950), p. 132.

CHAPTER 5

UTOPIA U.

In recent years there has been much heated discussion regarding the proper roles of the administration, the faculty, and the student body in the functioning of a liberal arts college. To my mind, however, these roles can be stated simply and succinctly: administrators should administrate, teachers should teach, and students should study. In this final chapter I want to describe a school in which each of the three constituent groups carries out its responsibilities conscientiously, with full appreciation of the high intellectual standards implicit in a sound liberal education. We shall call this ideal school "Utopia U."

Is Utopia U. a democratic institution? In one sense it is, for it is dedicated to providing citizens of a democracy with the necessary understanding and capability to make a success of their form of government. In another sense, however, Utopia U. is not democratic, for it is not governed by the principle of majority rule. Majority rule is a sound decision procedure only when no one can reasonably claim special competence in the matter being decided. But the essence of a college is that it affords an opportunity for students to learn from and be certified by those who do possess special competence, namely, the faculty. If the faculty had no such competence, what would qualify them to be teachers? And if the students had nothing to learn, why would they be students? Furthermore, what sense would there be in certifying a student's competence if the student himself chose the criteria of competence? That way lies educational anarchy. The academic expertise of the faculty provides the *raison d'être* for a college, and so at Utopia U. all decisions of educational policy are made in accord with the expert judgment of faculty.

To place such power in the hands of the faculty is not, however, to disregard student interests, for it is in students' interest to receive an education planned and supervised by those possessing the qualifications to make wise educational decisions. Of course, every member of the faculty has the responsibility to listen attentively to suggestions students may offer about the academic program. But a faculty worthy of respect responds only to student needs, not to student demands. A student may not know his own needs; that is why he is a student.

In order to become a member of the faculty at Utopia U., an individual must show promise as a teacher. Specifically, he must evidence a serious commitment to the ideals of liberal education and a deep concern for the intellectual growth of each of his students. He must be a knowledgeable individual, able to think clearly, speak comprehensibly, and write cogently, for he will be called upon both to communicate knowledge and to judge the skill with which others think, speak, and write. He must have the courage to defend his own beliefs and the open-mindedness to do justice to the beliefs he opposes. He must be sympathetic to those suffering the pains of genuine learning, but critical of those who are complacently putting forth less than their best effort. Finally, he must be aware of the special pitfalls inherent in his particular style of teaching.

This last point requires some elaboration. I have found it useful to distinguish between two types of teachers: one pushes the subject matter in front of him and one pulls the subject matter behind him. The latter uses his own personality to attract students and tries to transfer the students' interest from himself to the subject matter. The former minimizes his own personality and tries to interest students directly in the subject.[1]

One who pulls the subject behind him usually has little difficulty in arousing a student's interest, but his characteristic pitfall is the failure to effect the transfer of interest from teacher to subject matter. He may become a friend of the students but in so doing fail to teach them anything. As Sidney Hook has perceptively remarked, a teacher "must be friendly without becoming a friend, although he may pave the way for later friendship, for friendship is a mark of preference and expresses itself in indulgence, favors, and distinctions that unconsciously find an invidious form. . . . A teacher who becomes 'just one of the boys,' who courts popularity, who builds up personal loyalty in exchange for indulgent treatment, has missed his vocation. He should leave the classroom for professional politics."[2] But this is not to say that a teacher who pulls the subject behind him cannot be a superb instructor. Indeed, if he succeeds in transferring the students' interest from himself to the subject matter, he can exert a tremendous influence for the good on an enormous number of students, for such a teacher invariably attracts a great many devoted admirers who will follow wherever he leads, even down the rugged road of learning.

The one who pushes the subject in front of him need have no worry about misdirecting a student's interest; his worry is whether the student's interest will be aroused at all. The question of how to engage and maintain student interest was discussed in chapter two. What should be emphasized here is that the teacher has a responsibility to motivate his students. The content of a liberal education is of vital importance to members of a democracy, and what is important to an individual will be of interest if its significance is made clear. A teacher who fails to convey the point of what he is discussing sees his own inadequacy reflected in the eyes of his bored students. Obtaining a sound liberal education is difficult enough for a student interested in his work; for one who becomes bored the process is intolerable. Thus a teacher who pushes the subject in front of him had better be sure he presents his material interestingly, for a democracy that drives its students away from school will have to pay a high price for the widespread ignorance among its citizenry.

How does Utopia U. evaluate a faculty member's pedagogical skill? The most reliable way is for an expert to observe him while he teaches, and so at Utopia U. teachers are visited in their classrooms by other faculty members chosen as judges of teaching because of their own outstanding teaching ability, proven over the course of many years' experience. Though students may prepare a faculty evaluation booklet for their own use, their opinions play no formal role in the hiring or firing of faculty. Students know whether a teacher is engaging, but they cannot know whether he is presenting his material competently or whether years after graduation his methods of teaching will prove valuable. In any case, as Charles Frankel has pointed out, "Teaching is a professional relationship, not a popularity contest. To invite students to participate in the selection or promotion of their teachers . . . exposes the teacher to intimidation." [8]

But it is vital that a teacher not be intimidated by his students, for not only does good teaching require an instructor to evaluate his students' work honestly, but a vital part of his responsibility is to challenge a student's pet beliefs, expose his prejudices, and call into question his fundamental commitments. A teacher afraid of his students might just as well pack his briefcase and go home, for he cannot educate those whom he fears. A teacher must be safeguarded against threats by students or anyone else inside or outside the school, and so Utopia U. grants an instructor tenure as soon as he has clearly demonstrated pedagogic competence. The tenure system may occasionally protect a teacher who has lost some effectiveness, but that system is the best way I know to ensure teachers are not intimidated on account of their beliefs. And such intimidation must not be permitted, for where it festers good teaching is a virtual impossibility.

Having discussed the faculty at Utopia U. let us next consider the student body. The primary consideration for admission to Utopia U. is a deep-seated desire to learn. Within the financial resources of the School, all who exhibit such desire may enter. Those who come with especially weak academic backgrounds are placed in intensive remedial programs designed to enable a student to handle college-level work successfully. Entering Utopia U., however, is no guarantee of receiving the School's degree.

A student whose work is clearly unsatisfactory will be asked to leave, for as noted in the previous chapter, such a student is squandering his school's resources, wasting the time and energy of his teachers, and failing to contribute to, perhaps even interfering with, the education of his classmates. In short, Utopia U. is open to all who welcome and have a reasonable chance of meeting the challenges inherent in obtaining a sound liberal education.

Students at Utopia U. are working hard in order to obtain a sound liberal education, and to achieve their objective they must fulfill a variety of academic requirements. In the first two years of college, all students are expected to take a semester of English composition, a year's course integrating the physical sciences, a year's course integrating the biological sciences, a two-year course integrating the social sciences, world history, and American history, a semester of mathematics, a semester's course integrating logic, scientific method, and philosophy, a year of world literature, a semester of foreign literature in the original language, a semester of art, and a semester of music. These courses are not intended only for future scholars but are especially designed to make a significant contribution to every student's liberal education. Any of these requirements can be waived if a student demonstrates, by passing an equivalency examination, that he already possesses the knowledge and skills taught in a required area of study. During the last two years of college, all students must complete a specialization, either in a traditional field of scholarship such as English, history, or physics or in a more strictly vocational field such as journalism, business administration, or social work. Utopia U. offers as many such specializations as it can financially support, for different sorts of vocational plans require different sorts of specialized education.

We should note that formal education at Utopia U. most often takes place in lecture courses or seminars; comparatively little academic credit is available for independent study. Such study is all too often an excuse for students to avoid work and for faculty to avoid students. Scholars profitably discuss their research work with other scholars, and there seems no good reason why students cannot profitably discuss their research work with a teacher and other students. Even a student working on a lengthy term paper will find it highly useful to attend a weekly seminar in which his own work and the related work of his peers is critically examined by all. Of course, the work at Utopia U. is judged by rigorous intellectual standards, and the faculty are extremely conscientious about examination and grading procedures.

Some might argue at this point that although the students enrolled at Utopia U. may learn a great deal, they will become increasingly unhappy under the yoke of stiff academic requirements. This objection, however, is fundamentally mistaken. The most unhappy students I have ever met were those who found themselves in a leisurely atmosphere where they learned nothing, while the happiest students were those experiencing the joy of surmounting high intellectual barriers. John Gardner put the matter well when he said that "We fall into the error of thinking that happiness necessarily involves ease, diversion, tranquility—a state in which all of one's wishes are satisfied. For most people, happiness is not to be found in this vegetative state but in *striving toward meaningful goals*." [4] Challenge breeds interest and excitement. And if a student finds that by meeting educational challenges he is increasing his understanding of the world and broadening his intellectual horizons, he will take pride in his accomplishments and his school, and be eager to continue his work. Students acquiring new knowledge, new skills, and new interests in the classroom have little patience with those who need to find their excitement in the disruption of classes. Education provides the excitement at Utopia U.

What about the administration at Utopia U.? What is its role? Administrators are the caretakers and guardians of the educational mansion. They help to smooth its day-to-day operations while securing it against those who knowingly or unknowingly would undermine the very purposes for which it stands.

Apart from attending to the financial concerns of the School, perhaps the primary duty of the administration is to ensure an atmosphere in which faculty are free to inquire, publish, and teach, and students are free to inquire, study, and learn. Utopia U. is dedicated to the pursuit of knowledge; such pursuit may lead to dark corners where lie unpopular, controversial, even heretical opinions. But, as John Stuart Mill wrote, "the only way in which a human being can make some approach to knowing the whole of a subject is by hearing what can be said about it by persons of every variety of opinion, and studying all modes in which it can be looked at by ever character of mind. No wise man ever acquired his wisdom in any mode but this; nor is it in the nature of human intellect to become wise in any other manner." [5]

Utopia U's commitment to academic freedom is incompatible with the School's adopting any official stance on issues unrelated to its educational ideals. Free inquiry is impeded when certain opinions have been officially declared false and others true. The School is not in business to inform the public of what the majority of faculty or students consider the truth on any issue, be it mathematical, scientific, or political. At Utopia U., whether the ontological argument is sound or the Viet Nam War immoral is a matter for discussion, not decree.

The maintenance of free inquiry also requires that all points of view be entitled to a hearing. Students or faculty may invite any speaker they wish to the campus, no matter what heresy or orthodoxy he may espouse. And the School's administration has the job to ensure that no speaker, however controversial, is harassed or prevented from presenting his particular viewpoint.

The administration also has an obligation to make sure that no one, regardless of his proclaimed cause, is permitted to shut down college buildings, disrupt classes, or in any other way forcibly interfere with the School's normal educational processes. Free inquiry involves the clash of ideas, but there can be no clash of ideas where there is a clash of forces. It must be made clear to all that criminal behavior will not be tolerated simply because it happens to occur on a college campus.

Finally, Utopia U's administration has the responsibility of exerting firm leadership in the academic community by making its executive decisions in accordance with the School's commitment to the highest standards of intellectual accomplishment. This aspect of the administration's role is symbolized at commencement, when the President awards prizes, grants degrees, and addresses all faculty and students to encourage them in their mutual quest for excellence. Utopia U., it should be noted, has no embarrassment about singling out individuals to receive awards for outstanding academic achievement, for not only are such awards an added incentive for students to pursue their work diligently but also, as Jacques Barzun remarked, "we shall never have excellence unless we are willing to distinguish it in public from mediocrity." [6] It should be emphasized that a Utopia U. degree represents more than just payment of tuition fees or maintenance of residence requirements; it represents the recipient's mastery of the essentials of a sound liberal education. And that achievement ought to be a source of pride not only to the student and his family but also to the democracy whose future depends so heavily on the education of its citizens.

Of course, the most critical question remains unanswered: is Utopia U. a realistic possibility or merely an impractical vision? In short, has our society become so bogged down in the glorification of mediocrity that it cannot overcome the present eclipse of excellence? No one, I think, knows the answer to that question. But if the answer is in the negative—if requirements, examinations, grades, and standards no longer have a serious role in American college education—then we shall have only ourselves to blame as ignorance causes the decay of our democracy.

1. Many instructors engage to some extent in both these types of teaching.

2. Hook, pp. 230-231.

3. Charles Frankel, *Education and the Barricades* (New York: W. W. Norton & Company, 1968), pp. 30-31.

4. John W. Gardner, *Excellence: Can We Be Equal and Excellent Too?* (New York: Harper & Row, 1961), p. 149.

5. Mill, p. 25.

6. Barzun, p. 197.

www.ingramcontent.com/pod-product-compliance
Lightning Source LLC
Chambersburg PA
CBHW060645280326
41933CB00012B/2154